PREPARING
FOR
MARRIAGE

A Guide for Christian Couples

Edited by Donald J. Luther

PREPARING FOR MARRIAGE
A Guide for Christian Couples

First published as *Perspectives in Marriage*, copyright © 1988, 1992 ACTA.

Scripture quotations unless otherwise noted are from the New Revised Standard Version of the Bible, copyright © 1989 by the Division of Christian Education of the National Council of the Churches of Christ in the United States of America.

We wish to express our gratitude to Mary E. Buckley, Gregory F. Augustine Pierce, Ms. Elizabeth Bannon, Ms. Patricia Dondanville Berman, Rev. Thomas Hickey, Rev. Gerald Joyce, Mr. Chris Malone. Rev. Daniel Polizzi, Ms. Karen Skerrett, Mr. William Urbine and Mr. Daniel Wyatt for their contributions to the original ACTA publication.

Cover design: Catherine Reishus McLaughlin
Interior design: McCormick Creative/Nancy Condon

The paper used in this publication meets the minimum requirements of American National Standard for Information Sciences—Permanence of Paper for Printed Library Materials, ANSI Z329.48-1984. ∞™

Manufactured in the U.S.A.   AF 9-2569

04 03 02 01 00 99 98 97 6 7 8 9 10 11 12

CONTENTS

INTRODUCTION

Choosing to marry—to commit yourself entirely to another for your lifetime—may well be the most important decision you have made, or will make, in your life. Complete commitment to another is at the heart of your wedding preparation. So don't spend all your time before the wedding planning the reception, designing the rings, or furnishing your new home.

Although you probably had a course in school and participated in thousands of discussions about marriage, your perspective on marriage is bound to have changed. Now that you have made the decision to marry and have selected a special partner with whom you are planning to "take the plunge," a more in-depth consideration of marriage is necessary and appropriate.

This book is designed to help you take a good, long look at marriage—not just any marriage, but *your* marriage.

Preparing for Marriage contains thought-provoking exercises to help you think through and share your thoughts and feelings about marriage, its meaning, and its challenges. Don't merely complete the exercises and exchange them. Their value is found *after* the exchange, when you begin to probe, share feelings, question, and work to understand each other more deeply. The exercises are *not* scientific personality tests. They are tools that are designed to: (1) promote and stimulate conversation, (2) deepen mutual understanding, and (3) draw out insights and feelings about sensitive areas that otherwise might not be discussed.

There are two copies of some of the exercises so that each of you can tear one out, complete it, and then discuss them together. Other exercises are "discussion starters" for you to read and think about together.

Remember: The value of these exercises is in the conversations that follow them!

HOW DO YOU VIEW ME?—MAN'S PERSPECTIVE

You are invited to compare your view of yourself with your *partner's* view of you. The image we have of ourselves is not necessarily shared by even those near and dear to us.

DIRECTIONS

1. Tear this page from your book and mark list A by circling one, and *only one*, of the five dots on each horizontal line. Each of the five dots is keyed to the words above: very, somewhat, neutral, etc. Indicate the degree you feel most nearly describes your personality; in the first line you might circle "very excitable" or "somewhat calm." Then proceed to the next line.

2. Mark list B to describe your future spouse's personality traits.

3. Connect all the circled dots with a line.

4. Fold and tear on the vertical dotted line. Keep list A for yourself and give your partner list B. Your partner will do the same with her sheet.

5. Hold the sheets side by side, comparing first your views of yourself and then your views of each other. (The pattern of connected dots will aid this comparison.) Discuss the differences.

A. MAN ABOUT HIMSELF

	VERY	SOMEWHAT	NEUTRAL	SOMEWHAT	VERY	
calm	•	•	•	•	•	excitable
assertive	•	•	•	•	•	passive
reserved	•	•	•	•	•	affectionate
skeptical	•	•	•	•	•	trusting
extroverted	•	•	•	•	•	introverted
self-questioning	•	•	•	•	•	confident
procrastinating	•	•	•	•	•	compulsive
spendthrift	•	•	•	•	•	tightwad
happy-go-lucky	•	•	•	•	•	careful planner
realist	•	•	•	•	•	optimist
detached	•	•	•	•	•	sympathetic
social	•	•	•	•	•	private
serious	•	•	•	•	•	whimsical
relaxed	•	•	•	•	•	eager
critical	•	•	•	•	•	permissive
liberal	•	•	•	•	•	conservative
uncommunicative	•	•	•	•	•	communicative
self-sufficient	•	•	•	•	•	reliant
open	•	•	•	•	•	reticent
forceful	•	•	•	•	•	long-suffering
organized	•	•	•	•	•	disorganized
practical	•	•	•	•	•	dreamer
cautious	•	•	•	•	•	bold

B. MAN ABOUT WOMAN

	VERY	SOMEWHAT	NEUTRAL	SOMEWHAT	VERY	
calm	•	•	•	•	•	excitable
assertive	•	•	•	•	•	passive
reserved	•	•	•	•	•	affectionate
skeptical	•	•	•	•	•	trusting
extroverted	•	•	•	•	•	introverted
self-questioning	•	•	•	•	•	confident
procrastinating	•	•	•	•	•	compulsive
spendthrift	•	•	•	•	•	tightwad
happy-go-lucky	•	•	•	•	•	careful planner
realist	•	•	•	•	•	optimist
detached	•	•	•	•	•	sympathetic
social	•	•	•	•	•	private
serious	•	•	•	•	•	whimsical
relaxed	•	•	•	•	•	eager
critical	•	•	•	•	•	permissive
liberal	•	•	•	•	•	conservative
uncommunicative	•	•	•	•	•	communicative
self-sufficient	•	•	•	•	•	reliant
open	•	•	•	•	•	reticent
forceful	•	•	•	•	•	long-suffering
organized	•	•	•	•	•	disorganized
practical	•	•	•	•	•	dreamer
cautious	•	•	•	•	•	bold

CLUE EACH OTHER IN

Your partner has traits, qualities, and ways of acting that you especially prize and appreciate, and that you wish he or she would develop even more. But your partner is not a mind reader. When you tell him or her those qualities you find especially attractive, love will lead your partner to concentrate on them even more.

Read the qualities presented below. Pick out and list the seven you appreciate most about your partner in the order of their importance. Feel free to include other qualities not on this list—they might be the most important of all.

Sexually attractive

Flexible and open

Turns me on physically

Cares about people

Understanding

Affectionate

Patient with me

Makes me laugh

Dependable

Intelligent

Religious

Imaginative

Helps me feel secure

Is considerate

Hardworking

Is strong

Invites me to do new things

Doesn't blow up

Is interesting and alive

Cares about a home

Doesn't push me

Talks to me

Listens to me

Socially at ease

What I appreciate about you most is:

1. _____

2. _____

3. _____

4. _____

5. _____

6. _____

7. _____

HOW DO YOU VIEW ME?
—WOMAN'S PERSPECTIVE

You are invited to compare your view of yourself with your *partner's* view of you. The image we have of ourselves is not necessarily shared by even those near and dear to us.

DIRECTIONS

1. Tear this page from your book and mark list A by circling one, and *only one*, of the five dots on each horizontal line. Each of the five dots is keyed to the words above: very, somewhat, neutral, etc. Indicate the degree you feel most nearly describes your personality; in the first line you might circle "very excitable" or "somewhat calm." Then proceed to the next line.

2. Mark list B to describe your future spouse's personality traits.

3. Connect all the circled dots with a line.

4. Fold and tear on the vertical dotted line. Keep list A for yourself and give your partner list B. Your partner will do the same with her sheet.

5. Hold the sheets side by side, comparing first your views of yourself and then your views of each other. (The pattern of connected dots will aid this comparison.) Discuss the differences.

A. WOMAN ABOUT HERSELF

	VERY	SOMEWHAT	NEUTRAL	SOMEWHAT	VERY	
calm	•	•	•	•	•	excitable
assertive	•	•	•	•	•	passive
reserved	•	•	•	•	•	affectionate
skeptical	•	•	•	•	•	trusting
extroverted	•	•	•	•	•	introverted
self-questioning	•	•	•	•	•	confident
procrastinating	•	•	•	•	•	compulsive
spendthrift	•	•	•	•	•	tightwad
happy-go-lucky	•	•	•	•	•	careful planner
realist	•	•	•	•	•	optimist
detached	•	•	•	•	•	sympathetic
social	•	•	•	•	•	private
serious	•	•	•	•	•	whimsical
relaxed	•	•	•	•	•	eager
critical	•	•	•	•	•	permissive
liberal	•	•	•	•	•	conservative
uncommunicative	•	•	•	•	•	communicative
self-sufficient	•	•	•	•	•	reliant
open	•	•	•	•	•	reticent
forceful	•	•	•	•	•	long-suffering
organized	•	•	•	•	•	disorganized
practical	•	•	•	•	•	dreamer
cautious	•	•	•	•	•	bold

B. WOMAN ABOUT MAN

	VERY	SOMEWHAT	NEUTRAL	SOMEWHAT	VERY	
calm	•	•	•	•	•	excitable
assertive	•	•	•	•	•	passive
reserved	•	•	•	•	•	affectionate
skeptical	•	•	•	•	•	trusting
extroverted	•	•	•	•	•	introverted
self-questioning	•	•	•	•	•	confident
procrastinating	•	•	•	•	•	compulsive
spendthrift	•	•	•	•	•	tightwad
happy-go-lucky	•	•	•	•	•	careful planner
realist	•	•	•	•	•	optimist
detached	•	•	•	•	•	sympathetic
social	•	•	•	•	•	private
serious	•	•	•	•	•	whimsical
relaxed	•	•	•	•	•	eager
critical	•	•	•	•	•	permissive
liberal	•	•	•	•	•	conservative
uncommunicative	•	•	•	•	•	communicative
self-sufficient	•	•	•	•	•	reliant
open	•	•	•	•	•	reticent
forceful	•	•	•	•	•	long-suffering
organized	•	•	•	•	•	disorganized
practical	•	•	•	•	•	dreamer
cautious	•	•	•	•	•	bold

CLUE EACH OTHER IN

Your partner has traits, qualities, and ways of acting that you especially prize and appreciate, and that you wish he or she would develop even more. But your partner is not a mind reader. When you tell him or her those qualities you find especially attractive, love will lead your partner to concentrate on them even more.

Read the qualities presented below. Pick out and list the seven you appreciate most about your partner in the order of their importance. Feel free to include other qualities not on this list—they might be the most important of all.

Sexually attractive	Helps me feel secure
Flexible and open	Is considerate
Turns me on physically	Hardworking
Cares about people	Is strong
Understanding	Invites me to do new things
Affectionate	Doesn't blow up
Patient with me	Is interesting and alive
Makes me laugh	Cares about a home
Dependable	Doesn't push me
Intelligent	Talks to me
Religious	Listens to me
Imaginative	Socially at ease

What I appreciate about you most is:

1. _____

2. _____

3. _____

4. _____

5. _____

6. _____

7. _____

LOOK BEFORE YOU LEAP

If the following statement disturbs you, we are sorry. But marriage counselors are often asked, "What is the most common cause of marital breakups?" In all honesty some of them answer . . .

> "These two people should never have married in the first place—or, at least, they should never have married each other."

Most of you will build satisfactory marriages; many of you will build very happy marriages. For the few of you who might not do either, the following warning signs might well indicate whether you should have second thoughts. We will call them the fourteen "ifs."

1. You may be very deeply in love, but if you have known each other for less than three months, professionals say it is doubtful that you have been acquainted long enough to really *know* the person you plan to marry. Better give yourselves and the relationship more time.

2. If your partner has been really drunk or used drugs heavily three times in the past three weeks or about ten times in the past three or four months, he or she may have a problem that requires professional help. No marriage should begin if one partner is clearly unstable, troubled, and in need of professional help.

3. If your partner makes statements like: "I owe a great deal to mother. It's my duty to make her happy," and if such statements are coupled with behavior that makes it apparent that he or she will do almost anything to ensure parental approval, you should consider how close a relationship with in-laws a healthy marriage can sustain.

4. If your partner says things like: "I can't live without you; my life has no meaning apart from you; if I ever lost you I would kill myself," and if such statements are joined to very *obvious dependent behavior*, he or she may bring nothing to the relationship beyond deep draining needs. Being needed so desperately may flatter the ego for awhile, but if that's all there is, the relationship may become dull and draining.

5. If you have developed a pattern of quarrelling with, disappointing, seriously irritating, or hurting each other during the majority of times that you have been together in the last three months, perhaps you are trying subconsciously to tell each other something. Think about it. Marriage will not erase this type of discontent.

6. If many of the significant, mature people in your life—parents, relatives, teachers, and especially good friends who love you—*indicate that you may be making a mistake*, you should take pause. If people muster up the courage to comment (in words or otherwise) on another's decision, weigh their opinions or nonverbal reactions carefully.

7. If some very *serious problem* has occurred in the past few weeks, and if it is definitely troubling you, and if you have not had an opportunity to work it through, then either confront the problem or think about postponing the wedding.

8. If your financial situation is uncertain, and there appears to be no means of correcting it in the near future, don't pass it off because "we're in love." Statistics show that financial problems are a significant factor in the dissolution of at least 40 percent of all marriages. Although money does not buy happiness, lack of money can cause a great deal of stress and unhappiness.

9. If all of your friends are marrying and you feel pressured to do the same, don't! You can sustain any amount of societal or peer pressure to avoid an unhappy life.

10. If you feel that having become sexually involved commits you to marrying each other despite serious problems in your relationship, don't. A good marriage is predicated on maturity and responsibility, not on sexual involvement that may not be founded on love.

11. If both of you are eighteen years of age or under, your potential for divorce is three and a half times greater than that of people who are twenty-one years of age and over.

12. If you are marrying because you just *have to get out of the house*, you will ultimately hurt only yourself if marriage is merely a means of asserting your freedom or "getting back" at your parents for past hurts. Moving out of the house might be very appropriate, but should marriage be the excuse or the way?

13. If you are a pregnant couple (it does take two!), then slow down, think, talk, ponder, and pray. Neither pregnancy itself nor the fear of any social stigma that pregnancy might cause are good reasons to marry. Ask yourselves whether you would really marry one another if there were no pregnancy.

14. If your backgrounds or cultures differ so greatly that strong differences of opinion about important matters have already occurred, the difficulties will more than likely increase when you marry. Further, if one partner consistently compromises and the other never does, resentment might eventually build up on both sides. You should be able to meet one another at least halfway.

NOTE: No one can predict that your marriage will fail or succeed, and none of these warning signs spells absolute disaster. The risk that you take is part of the adventure of marriage. But, if you decide to take that risk, you must first consider the odds. Are they in your favor? If not, you might be taking a far greater risk than you should.

Please do not panic, bury your head in the sand, or hit the road. But, do think it over and talk it over. Make certain that your decision to marry is made responsibly, with good judgment. You might want to ask advice from a qualified, unbiased person, such as a pastor, priest, or married person.

Although marriage is a wonderful state, it is also a life-long task that should be given careful consideration before a lasting decision is made or binding action taken. You owe it to one another to be honest about your feelings and your situation. *Only good can come of it.*

DISCOVERING EACH OTHER

This gentle exercise will help elicit important feelings that lovers might wish to discuss.

A

Use this column to answer the following items as directly as you can.

B

Now, put yourself in your partner's shoes and jot down the answers you think he or she has written under column A.

PLEASE WORK ALONE

1. The reason I love you

_____

_____

_____

2. My strongest quality

_____

_____

_____

3. My greatest weakness

_____

_____

_____

4. My usual means of avoiding conflict

_____

_____

_____

5. My biggest worry

_____

_____

_____

6. A sensitive area in which I have trouble taking criticism

_____

_____

_____

7. My greatest interest and concern other than our relationship

_____

_____

_____

8. My definition of sexual love

9. My greatest fear about my upcoming marriage

10. The biggest adjustment I'll have to make in our first year of marriage

11. What describes us best as a couple

12. The thing I find most difficult (unpleasant, confusing) to talk about

13. Five years from now we'll be

14. The number of children I want

After you have completed the exercise, exchange papers with your partner, relax, and compare them. Discuss your answers. Do any surprise you? Do you disagree with any of the answers? Are any especially interesting or thought provoking?

DISCOVERING EACH OTHER

This gentle exercise will help elicit important feelings that lovers might wish to discuss.

	A	**B**
	Use this column to answer the following items as directly as you can.	Now, put yourself in your partner's shoes and jot down the answers you think he or she has written under column A.
		PLEASE WORK ALONE
1. The reason I love you		
2. My strongest quality		
3. My greatest weakness		
4. My usual means of avoiding conflict		
5. My biggest worry		
6. A sensitive area in which I have trouble taking criticism		
7. My greatest interest and concern other than our relationship		

8. My definition of sexual love

_____   _____

_____   _____

_____   _____

9. My greatest fear about my upcoming marriage

_____   _____

_____   _____

_____   _____

10. The biggest adjustment I'll have to make in our first year of marriage

_____   _____

_____   _____

_____   _____

11. What describes us best as a couple

_____   _____

_____   _____

_____   _____

12. The thing I find most difficult (unpleasant, confusing) to talk about

_____   _____

_____   _____

_____   _____

13. Five years from now we'll be

_____   _____

_____   _____

_____   _____

14. The number of children I want

_____   _____

_____   _____

_____   _____

After you have completed the exercise, exchange papers with your partner, relax, and compare them. Discuss your answers. Do any surprise you? Do you disagree with any of the answers? Are any especially interesting or thought provoking?

PLAYING SOLOMON

1. Peter and I are not very religious, and neither of us has been to church for quite awhile. However, both his parents and mine are "old school" and will be crushed if we don't have a church wedding.

When we went to the church to make arrangements, we had a hassled discussion with the pastor, who said he wouldn't preside at our wedding because we have no faith commitment. I'll admit that this idea of a relationship between faith and marriage doesn't do anything for us, but we are baptized Christians! The pastor gave us reading materials that look pretty dull and said he'd be willing to talk with us again.

What shall we do? Tell him what he wants to hear? Decide we'll have a civil ceremony, or what?

What is the pastor's point? To what does this couple object? Do you think a compromise is possible or appropriate?

2. If my mother-in-law makes one more comment on my cooking or housekeeping, I think I'll scream. Because she has nothing to do, she drops in two or three times a week and tells me what's wrong with my recipes; tells me why I should change furniture polish; tells me why the plant won't grow in that corner; and also tells me why I shouldn't spend money to have the laundry done. She never speaks a word that doesn't direct or imply criticism toward me.

I keep telling Larry. He says he knows that his mother can be a pain sometimes, but he also says that I am too sensitive. Besides, he adds, I'm a big girl and can fight my own battles.

What do you suggest?

3. We've been married for five months, and Susan supports trust, openness, and honesty in our marriage. I must admit that this approach is working out pretty well for us. Lately, though, she's been telling me about old boyfriends and has been probing about girls I was involved with.

I used to be a bit of a swinger and was sexually involved with some of the women I dated. Part of me wants to open up and tell her about it, if only to let her know how much greater she is in every way. But another part of me says to keep my mouth shut!

What she doesn't know won't hurt her or come back to haunt me later! How much do I tell?

In what kinds of situations is it helpful to "tell all"? When could it be harmful?

4. We've been married eleven weeks, and Paul has just told me he plans to spend four or five nights a month out with the boys, bowling or just drinking and talking. He says we both need private lives and our own circle of friends and that I should make similar arrangements.

I can understand occasional nights out, but this planning to be apart bothers me. I married him to be with him and to do things together. Besides, my girl friends don't go out much without their husbands.

Why might she be reacting to the "planning"? What's better for a couple—separate friends or only mutual ones?

5. When I came home from shopping last Saturday, Randy informed me that his sister had just called and that he had agreed to go over for drinks and hamburgers in their backyard. I like his sister very much, but I feel my husband has no right making social commitments without checking with me first. He could have easily have said, "I'll see if Julie has anything planned and call you back." This is about the third time that Randy has done something like this during the nine months we've been married.

When we talked about it, he said, "We had no plans, and you shouldn't be disturbed in an informal situation like this. If you really didn't want to go, it would have been easy to call and cancel."

Is Randy off base, or is Julie too rigid? What might prevent these kinds of problems for a couple?

6. About the only thing that bugs me about my fiance is that he makes no plans. When he calls, his second sentence is always, "What do you want to do?" When I say, "I don't know," we flounder for thirty minutes, and we get irritated and do nothing.

I think it's the man's responsibility to make definite suggestions and plans. He says there just aren't that many things he likes to do and that I'm the one that likes variety.

Is this the kind of impasse that could lead to boredom with each other or other problems in marriage? What should they do?

7. Our wedding is only a couple of months away, and I have a problem. Anytime something irritates or displeases Jennifer, she withdraws. By now, although I can tell the mood immediately, it's always an uphill battle: First, to get her to admit there is a problem, then, to find out what it is, and, finally, to begin to discuss it reasonably.

I come from a big family, and I can handle noise and fights, but silence frustrates and angers me. She says she just doesn't like to argue, and if I would just ignore her moods, we would get along better. She says I push too much to find out what she is thinking. I say ignoring her in these moods would be like ignoring a booby trap.

What can a partner's silence communicate? How could he approach Jennifer?

8. My wife is great, and I love her. Lately, however, she's into the whole woman's movement, which is fine with me in theory. But somehow, it has turned me off. It's even reached the bedroom. I know it's my problem, but it's affecting our relationship. I don't want Judy to be passive and submissive. But I can't seem to deal with this assertive and aggressive person with whom I suddenly find myself living.

What do you think he is feeling? Do you agree that it is "his problem"? What would you suggest he say to Judy?

9. Before we were married, we both agreed to delay having children so we could save money. Tonight, on the way home from my nephew's baptism, Michele mentioned how nice it might be to have a baby. It's not that I don't like kids. As a matter of fact, while I was holding my nephew, I really liked the feeling. And Michele would be a fantastic mother. But something says, "Tom, are you really ready to take on that kind of responsibility?" I don't know how to answer.

What are responsible reasons for having children? How does a couple know when they're ready?

10. During our courtship and engagement, I really liked Dan's easygoing manner. No matter what, he remained cool, calm, and collected. However, now that we've been married awhile, this easygoing attitude is starting to irritate me. At times, I wish he would blow up so I would know what's bothering him. I even feel that he's letting me make all the decisions. Sometime I'd love to hear him say, "Lisa, this is what we're going to do!" Should I thank my lucky stars that I married a guy like Dan? Or could something be seriously wrong?

How do you think Lisa views Dan's feelings towards her? Why is a quality she once liked in Dan something that irritates her now?

11. Tom and Sheila have been married seven years. Sheila has been working three days a week as a substitute teacher. She enjoys it and is very good at it. Her mother stays with their two little girls.

Now from a field of several hundred teachers, Sheila and eleven others have been selected to staff a new experimental school. The offer means going full-time at a very good salary. If Sheila takes the job she and Tom will have to purchase a second car because the new school is quite a bit further away.

Sheila is eager to try it, but Tom has reservations. He is working hard at his job and he thinks she should wait to tackle a career until the children are older. Sheila suspects that part of Tom's problem is that she would be making more money than he.

What would you advise?

12. Although my husband and I communicate with one another fairly well, sex is one area about which we just can't seem to talk. Lately, it has become a source of real tension. I know Todd wants to please me, but he always seems to assume what pleases me. He takes any sign of affection on my part to mean intercourse. If I indicate no, he pouts and sulks. Sometimes I have the feeling that he has an unrealistic ideal about how he should be as a lover. I can't go on like this much longer. Where do I begin?

Why is it so hard to talk about sex sometimes?

SHARING OUR FAITH VISION

Sharing religious attitudes, concerns, and questions with one another prior to marriage can have a very important effect on your respect for and understanding of each other. Religious faith can bring strength to your marriage; shared religious beliefs can increase the strength of marital love and the marital relationship.

Before you share your religious beliefs and attitudes, it might be worthwhile to clarify your thoughts in writing by answering the questions below. Share your feelings as openly and as freely as you can. If any of your responses or your discussions with one another raise concerns, it might also be worthwhile to initiate discussions with your pastor or priest.

1. When I pray, I _____

2. When I pray, I pray about _____

_____

3. One positive religious or spiritual experience I've had is _____

_____

_____

_____

4. A religious or spiritual experience that has turned me off is _____

_____

_____

_____

_____

5. On a scale of 1–10 (10 being most religious), I would rate myself this religious:_____

6. How satisfied are you with the level of religious intensity indicated in question 5?_____

7. I hope to share my faith and beliefs with my future spouse by_____

_____

_____

_____

_____

8. My reasons for marrying in the church are _____

_____

_____

9. My faith helps me in my life and marriage by _____

_____

_____

10. I contribute to the life of my church by _____

_____

_____

11. In terms of my marriage, I would like to ask God for _____

_____

_____

12. Some of my questions, doubts, and confusions about religion are _____

_____

_____

_____

13. (*If you are from different religious backgrounds:*) Sharing my faith with my partner will benefit
our marriage by

_____

_____

_____

14. (*If you are from different religious backgrounds:*) Some potential religious questions that might
create problems for us are

_____

_____

_____

_____

SHARING OUR FAITH VISION

Sharing religious attitudes, concerns, and questions with one another prior to marriage can have a very important effect on your respect for and understanding of each other. Religious faith can bring strength to your marriage; shared religious beliefs can increase the strength of marital love and the marital relationship.

Before you share your religious beliefs and attitudes, it might be worthwhile to clarify your thoughts in writing by answering the questions below. Share your feelings as openly and as freely as you can. If any of your responses or your discussions with one another raise concerns, it might also be worthwhile to initiate discussions with your pastor or priest.

1. When I pray, I _____

2. When I pray, I pray about _____

_____

3. One positive religious or spiritual experience I've had is _____

_____

_____

_____

4. A religious or spiritual experience that has turned me off is _____

_____

_____

_____

_____

5. On a scale of 1–10 (10 being most religious), I would rate myself this religious:_____

6. How satisfied are you with the level of religious intensity indicated in question 5?_____

7. I hope to share my faith and beliefs with my future spouse by_____

_____

_____

_____

_____

_____

8. My reasons for marrying in the church are _____

_____

_____

9. My faith helps me in my life and marriage by _____

_____

_____

10. I contribute to the life of my church by _____

_____

_____

11. In terms of my marriage, I would like to ask God for _____

_____

_____

12. Some of my questions, doubts and confusions about religion are _____

_____

_____

_____

13. (*If you are from different religious backgrounds:*) Sharing my faith with my partner will benefit our marriage by

_____

_____

_____

14. (*If you are from different religious backgrounds:*) Some potential religious questions that might create problems for us are

_____

_____

_____

_____

TWO FAITHS, ONE LOVE

Many marriages today involve two people from different religious backgrounds. This might include two Christians from different denominations, two people from totally different faiths, or even two people of the same religious tradition where one person's faith is very fervent and one's is not. Such couples usually realize—and official teaching of most religions have long insisted—that such "interfaith" marriages can pose special dangers.

Interfaith couples who do not deal with their religious differences may end up avoiding all religious questions and drifting into spiritual indifference, thereby losing an essential part of their individual lives and a major source of a richer life together. This indifference confuses their children, who do not know what to believe.

If you do not share the same religious beliefs and practices, you will have to work and pray hard to realize the potential special blessings of your marriage. Rather than ignoring your differences, honor them. Here are some suggestions:

- Encourage your partner's own religious pursuits and practices. Help each other keep in touch with the sources of grace and inspiration that each finds most useful. These practices will strengthen each partner's sense of self and enrich and benefit the relationship.

- Attend the other's worship services occasionally. Try to understand your partner's faith life. As a joint statement of Catholic, Protestant, and Jewish leaders puts it, "This attendance is in no sense a compromise. Love requires knowledge of the beloved."

- Try to get to know and understand some of your partner's fellow congregation members.

- If there are social groups or study clubs affiliated with your individual congregations that hold some interest for you, become involved together. Sometimes you might wish to attend special events jointly, like conferences or retreats of ecumenical celebrations.

- Consider your religious observance during the first few weeks of marriage. How will you schedule your time, breakfast, and transportation so you can attend services? After a while, convenient patterns will develop, but some forethought might be required at first.

- Learn to pray together with some regularity. Pray about your lives, your hopes, and your needs; pray for the people dear to you, for those in great need, and about some of the critical questions facing all of us today. Determine some of the occasions, some of the times of the day or week, when you can pray together.

- Consider using some prayers from each partner's faith tradition, some that you hold in common, and even new ones that you create to express special meanings for you and your marriage. In addition, there are many new, well-designed books of prayer and meditation that both of you will find very nourishing.

- Consider the religious rituals and customs that could be woven into your family life. Perhaps those that surround holy days from each of your traditions or nonreligious holidays such as Thanksgiving and Memorial Day might be a good place to start. Make a list of customs that have meaning for each of you. Discuss the various ways your families handled holidays and celebrations and see which ones might be suitable for your new family. Rituals give depth and richness to our lives because they remind us of meanings beyond daily routine. They don't just happen, however; you must work at them.

- Become involved as a couple in some charitable or service-oriented projects assisting the poor, the aged, children, and others. This could be a manifestation of your shared, but different, faiths.

- Confront the problem of the religious upbringing of your children honestly and early in your marriage. Realize that no perfect solution exists, but bear in mind that children require a consistent faith that tells them the meaning of the world. They need symbols, prayers, and practices that allow that faith to take root and have expression.

PLEASE LISTEN TO ME

When I ask you to listen to me
and you start giving advice,
you have not done what I asked.

When I ask you to listen to me
and you begin to tell me
why I shouldn't feel that way,
you are telling me to deny my feelings.

When I ask you to listen to me
and you feel you have to do something
to solve my problems,
you have failed me,
(strange as that may seem).

Listen.

All I ask is that you listen.

Not talk or do,
just hear me.

The giving of advice
can never take the place
of the giving of yourself.

I'm not helpless,
or hopeless!

When you do something for me
that I need to do for myself
you contribute to my fear
. . . and weakness.

But when you accept the simple fact
that I do feel what I feel
(no matter how irrational that may seem to you),
then I quit trying to convince you
and can get on with trying to understand
what's behind my feelings.

And when that's clear,
the answers are obvious.

And you know what?
Your listening made that possible.

Feelings make sense
when we understand
what's behind them.

Perhaps that's why prayer works
—sometimes—
for people,
because God is still
and doesn't give advice
or try to fix things.

God just listens
and lets you work it out
for yourself,
staying your "silent partner."

So please listen and just hear me,
and we can both keep in mind
that there are important times in our lives
when we just need to be heard

Not cured.

Author Unknown

THE BELLS ARE RINGING

Although courtship is a carefree, happy time for most couples, the actual preparation for the wedding can often bring problems to an otherwise harmonious relationship. It's safe to say that planning a wedding can be difficult. To be successful at it, you must negotiate with each other, with your families, and with vendors, and you must implement a number of mutual decisions. The manner in which these decisions are made may provide valuable clues to the way in which you will approach other decisions later on in marriage.

Listed below are comments made by couples like yourselves who were planning their weddings. Working together, check off those that reflect and those that do not reflect your approach to your wedding. Discuss your responses and how they reflect a decision-making style that may continue in your marriage.

	REFLECTS	DOES NOT REFLECT
A. My mother will handle everything.	_____	_____
B. We have divided the work evenly. She's ordering the flowers, etc., I'll choose the band, etc.	_____	_____
C. He has left everything to me, because he feels that I know how everything should be.	_____	_____
D. My mother and I have organized most of it, with occasional suggestions from my future spouse.	_____	_____
E. We have both been so busy that we really haven't had a chance to talk with each other to see if we have done what we agreed to do.	_____	_____
F. We talked about the kind of wedding we wanted, but our mothers are actually carrying out our plans.	_____	_____
G. She had the overall ideas for the day itself. I tried to fill in with different ways to do it or how much to spend on food and matters like that.	_____	_____
H. My fiancee and her sister literally took over what were to be our joint plans.	_____	_____

	REFLECTS	DOES NOT REFLECT

I. We decided how we wanted it, but we needed to compromise in a few places after her parents indicated their financial limitations or after we realized our own financial limitations.

J. My fiance travels a lot with his business, so he told me to do what I want.

K. His sister just got married, and his family has offered to organize things for us, too.

L. I think she's going overboard in many ways, but what can I say?

M. Frequently, I would suggest a song or reading for the wedding, but he would not like it. Or, according to him, I'd want to invite too many of my relatives and friends.

N. My mother really enjoyed planning our wedding until too many people started to interfere.

O. We set a financial limit and juggled different options until we found a plan that worked.

P. Our ideas about whether we want it big or small, formal or informal, morning or evening, are so completely different.

In discussing your responses, you might ask the following questions.

1. Do we work well together?_____

2. Are we avoiding or accepting responsibility?

_____

3. What is our decision-making style?

_____

4. Does a division of labor exist according to sex?

_____

5. Are we taking control of our own lives and our life together?

_____

6. How might future joint projects resemble this one? (For example, decorating and furnishing a house or apartment, planning a vacation, doing income tax, entertaining.)

_____

_____

_____

_____

As you respond to each of these questions, consider whether this is the way you want it to be.

FIGHTING WITHOUT FIGHTING

While fighting with your partner is not always bad, it's not exactly pleasant either, and it's certainly not what you are getting married to do. First of all, some things are just not worth arguing about. Remember, it's "for better or worse." You also need to learn now—before the wedding—the difference between the negotiable and the non-negotiable for both you and your partner.

Still, plenty of serious issues over the years will produce conflict. It is important for both of you to stand up for what you believe and to feel that you are getting what you expect from your relationship. Here are some suggestions for healthy, noncombative conflict resolution.

Ground Rules for Conflict Resolution

- Face the problem, disagreement, or difference of opinion squarely. It's not going to go away just because you don't talk about it.

- Try to understand your partner's point of view. Listen intently to what he or she is really saying—and why. Ask nonthreatening and non-blaming questions to clarify the key points of disagreement.

- Respond in an honest, yet caring way.

- Tell your partner how you feel, and allow him or her to do the same, even if the feelings are negative ones (like resentment, anxiety, anger, guilt). It's better to get those feelings out on the table where the other person can understand them rather than trying to guess what they are.

- Your partner is not the cause of your emotions, so you cannot expect him or her to "fix" how you're feeling or vice versa.

- Accept your share of the responsibility for coping with any conflict. Don't always leave it up to your partner to raise uncomfortable issues or propose solutions.

- Be willing to explore compromises or workable alternatives. It's not necessary—or even desirable—that one side "win" a conflict. Try to figure out a way that both of you get at least part of your needs met.

- Take steps, however small, to begin to implement the agreement you have come to together. There's nothing like a little change in the situation to make both sides feel better, and there's nothing worse than talking about a problem and having nothing happen as a result.

- Set a definite time for review to see if the issue needs further discussion or work.

FIGHTING FAIR

To presume that you will not argue after you are married is idealistic; it simply is not true. You *will* argue. And many psychologists would say that a good argument is often healthy because it promotes dialogue (couples *listen* and *talk* with one another) and good communication.

However, if they are to be fair and fruitful, marital arguments should follow certain ground rules. Hopefully, the goal of an argument is to solve a problem, not destroy the other person. While avoiding argument at all costs is unhealthy and stifling, arguing without certain positive guidelines can be destructive and disheartening. Here are a few tips.

GROUND RULES

- Listen to your partner. Give each other the opportunity to speak and to be heard, and don't dominate the discussion.

- Stick to the issues at hand. Dredging up past hurts or problems, whether real or perceived, is not helpful.

- Always complete the argument. To walk away angry or postpone the discussion indefinitely can cause more problems.

- Don't sling mud. Avoid sarcasm and name-calling. Use of phrases such as "stupid jerk," "fat slob," "drunken bum," or "lazy lump" only serves to hurt and incite more anger.

- Never use physical violence.

- Never threaten to withdraw love or sex.

- Avoid the "silent treatment." Nothing gets solved this way.

- When you are wrong, admit it.

- Don't make a scene. Never deliberately embarrass each other or others by arguing in front of other family members or in public. Keep your arguments private.

- Make up and mean it. Bitterness and grudges will undermine your relationship.

TRY, TRY AGAIN

Few things are more frustrating for a couple than trying to solve a simple problem together. Neither of you can fathom why the other does not recognize how wise and reasonable you are, concur with the solution you propose, and get on with other, more important, things.

The following exercise is an opportunity to take a look at how you come across to each other when you're in the middle of a "fight" or even a "spirited discussion." Together, choose one conflict the two of you have had recently that is still not resolved.

Then, working separately, try to remember your perception of how each of you handled it.

For each of the 10 questions in section A, put an "I" in the space before each response that you feel most closely describes your reactions and "Y" in the space before each response that you feel most closely describes your partner's reactions during your recent conflict. (You may fill in the same space for both of you on some or all of the questions.)

Section A: During this particular conflict, I felt that you (Y) and I (I):

1. _____ denied that a problem existed.

   _____ exaggerated the importance of the problem.

   _____ faced the problem squarely.

2. _____ heard what the other was saying.

   _____ ignored the other side.

3. _____ stuck to the point.

   _____ brought up extraneous issues.

4. _____ refused to discuss.

   _____ sought to explore the issue.

5. _____ held back.

   _____ poured forth feelings (especially negative ones).

6. _____ did / _____ did not accept responsibility for coping with the conflict.

7. _____ tried to compromise or create alternative solutions.

   _____ left all the suggestions to the other person.

8. _____ blamed someone else for causing the conflict.

   _____ accepted ownership of the difficulty.

9. _____ recognized what is possible.

   _____ held to unrealistic expectations.

10. _____ dealt with the conflict constructively.

    _____ kept harping on the same points.

Come together and compare your answers, discussing any surprises or differences in your perceptions. Finally, discuss each of the five steps listed in section B and see if they would help you actually resolve this particular conflict. If you think they would, then try them!

Section B: What would happen if we . . .

1. listed at least three possible options for resolving the current conflict?

2. discussed each option and then chose one together?

3. told each other how we felt about this decision?

4. tried to implement the decision?

5. agreed to discuss the matter again in two weeks?

ON OUR WORST BEHAVIOR

Here are ten behaviors that are often used to express or respond to anger or negative feelings during fights or disagreements. In each case, check if it characterizes you, your partner, neither of you, or both of you.

Then share your answers with each other. First, look for places where your perceptions differ and discuss why. Then, where you do agree on the nature of your behavior, discuss how productive the behaviors are and which ones you might want to change.

	ME	YOU	NEITHER	BOTH
Silence				
Blaming				
Yelling				
Pouting				
Sarcasm				
Avoidance				
Appeasement				
Crying				
Threatening				
Physical Violence				

TRY, TRY AGAIN

F ew things are more frustrating for a couple than trying to solve a simple problem together. Neither of you can fathom why the other does not recognize how wise and reasonable you are, concur with the solution you propose, and get on with other, more important, things.

The following exercise is an opportunity to take a look at how you come across to each other when you're in the middle of a "fight" or even a "spirited discussion." Together, choose one conflict the two of you have had recently that is still not resolved.

Then, working separately, try to remember your perception of how each of you handled it.

For each of the 10 questions in section A, put an "I" in the space before each response that you feel most closely describes your reactions and "Y" in the space before each response that you feel most closely describes your partner's reactions during your recent conflict. (You may fill in the same space for both of you on some or all of the questions.)

Section A: During this particular conflict, I felt that you (Y) and I (I):

1. _____ denied that a problem existed.

   _____ exaggerated the importance of the problem.

   _____ faced the problem squarely.

2. _____ heard what the other was saying.

   _____ ignored the other side.

3. _____ stuck to the point.

   _____ brought up extraneous issues.

4. _____ refused to discuss.

   _____ sought to explore the issue.

5. _____ held back.

   _____ poured forth feelings (especially negative ones).

6. _____ did / _____ did not accept responsibility for coping with the conflict.

7. _____ tried to compromise or create alternative solutions.

   _____ left all the suggestions to the other person.

8. _____ blamed someone else for causing the conflict.

   _____ accepted ownership of the difficulty.

9. _____ recognized what is possible.

   _____ held to unrealistic expectations.

10. _____ dealt with the conflict constructively.

   _____ kept harping on the same points.

Come together and compare your answers, discussing any surprises or differences in your perceptions. Finally, discuss each of the five steps listed in section B and see if they would help you actually resolve this particular conflict. If you think they would, then try them!

Section B: What would happen if we . . .

1. listed at least three possible options for resolving the current conflict?

2. discussed each option and then chose one together?

3. told each other how we felt about this decision?

4. tried to implement the decision?

5. agreed to discuss the matter again in two weeks?

ON OUR WORST BEHAVIOR

ere are ten behaviors that are often used to express or respond to anger or negative feelings during fights or disagreements. In each case, check if it characterizes you, your partner, neither of you, or both of you.

Then share your answers with each other. First, look for places where your perceptions differ and discuss why. Then, where you do agree on the nature of your behavior, discuss how productive the behaviors are and which ones you might want to change.

	ME	YOU	NEITHER	BOTH
Silence				
Blaming				
Yelling				
Pouting				
Sarcasm				
Avoidance				
Appeasement				
Crying				
Threatening				
Physical Violence				

SEX AND SEXUALITY

The more open and honest you and your partner are about your feelings and attitudes toward sex, the more fulfilling your overall relationship will be. Granted, sex is not the easiest subject to discuss openly—primarily because almost everyone experiences some anxiety when trying to verbalize feelings about sex. Although a natural aspect of human nature, sex is not simple: it involves roles, gender, physiology, emotions, and mystery. No one has all the right answers, so you need not be experienced to be able to discuss sex—just open to discussion and willing to listen.

To engage in open dialogue about sex, you must first understand yourself as a sexual being; that is, what has influenced you? How do you feel about sex? How do you feel about your partner sexually?

The questions in this exercise are designed to assist you in an honest appraisal of your sexual self. Jot down your responses and share them with your partner. Then, *listen* to each other.

QUESTIONS

Do you think that sex is: fun, frightening, threatening, pleasurable, exciting, satisfying, holy, expressive of your relationship, other? Give two descriptions that characterize your feelings about sex.

_____

_____

What are your feelings about your body?

_____

_____

What are your needs for affection?

_____

_____

How affectionate are you?

_____

_____

How comfortable are you when you touch and are touched?

_____

_____

What events and attitudes from your past have influenced your sexual behaviors and attitudes?

_____

_____

What memories or hang-ups (if any) must you work through to become comfortable
and confident with your sexuality?

_____

_____

Do you find anything offensive or vulgar about sex?

_____

_____

What do you need most from your sexual relationship?

_____

_____

As a sexual partner, a woman should . . .

_____

_____

As a sexual partner, a man should . . .

_____

_____

What circumstances do you find most exciting sexually?

_____

_____

When would you not want to have sex?

_____

Do you find any specific sexual acts immoral (improper) in marriage? Do you have any hesitations or reservations about sex?

_____

What worries you about sex in your marriage?

_____

_____

What do you look forward to sexually in your marriage?

_____

_____

What do you think your marital sex life will be like in ten years?

_____

_____

What do you find physically attractive about your partner?

_____

_____

What do you think your partner finds physically attractive about you?

_____

_____

_____

SEX AND SEXUALITY

The more open and honest you and your partner are about your feelings and attitudes toward sex, the more fulfilling your overall relationship will be. Granted, sex is not the easiest subject to discuss openly—primarily because almost everyone experiences some anxiety when trying to verbalize feelings about sex. Although a natural aspect of human nature, sex is not simple: it involves roles, gender, physiology, emotions, and mystery. No one has all the right answers, so you need not be experienced to be able to discuss sex—just open to discussion and willing to listen.

To engage in open dialogue about sex, you must first understand yourself as a sexual being; that is, what has influenced you? How do you feel about sex? How do you feel about your partner sexually?

The questions in this exercise are designed to assist you in an honest appraisal of your sexual self. Jot down your responses and share them with your partner. Then, *listen* to each other.

QUESTIONS

Do you think that sex is: fun, frightening, threatening, pleasurable, exciting, satisfying, holy, expressive of your relationship, other? Give two descriptions that characterize your feelings about sex.

_____

_____

What are your feelings about your body?

_____

_____

What are your needs for affection?

_____

_____

How affectionate are you?

_____

_____

How comfortable are you when you touch and are touched?

_____

_____

What events and attitudes from your past have influenced your sexual behaviors and attitudes?

_____

_____

What memories or hang-ups (if any) must you work through to become comfortable and confident with your sexuality?

_____

_____

Do you find anything offensive or vulgar about sex?

_____

_____

What do you need most from your sexual relationship?

_____

_____

As a sexual partner, a woman should . . .

_____

_____

As a sexual partner, a man should . . .

_____

_____

What circumstances do you find most exciting sexually?

_____

_____

When would you not want to have sex?

_____

Do you find any specific sexual acts immoral (improper) in marriage? Do you have any hesitations or reservations about sex?

_____

What worries you about sex in your marriage?

_____

_____

What do you look forward to sexually in your marriage?

_____

_____

What do you think your marital sex life will be like in ten years?

_____

_____

What do you find physically attractive about your partner?

_____

_____

What do you think your partner finds physically attractive about you?

_____

_____

BIRTH CONTROL

The fundamental concerns of birth control are the prevention of unplanned pregnancies and a measure of choice in family planning. However, beyond that, different needs and life-styles play a part in selecting the method(s) that is (are) satisfactory for both partners. A consultation with your health care provider, preferably as a couple, will help with any of the technical questions you may have. Remember, sexual intimacy, from a gentle, sensitive touch to intercourse, is an expression of your love for one another. Techniques and methods are meant to serve that expression. Given that, select the method that is right for you.

The following birth control methods require a doctor's prescription:

- the birth control pill
- the implantable contraceptive (approved by the FDA in 1991)
- the intrauterine device (IUD)
- the diaphragm and cervical cap

Methods which are available over-the-counter include:

- condoms
- contraceptive sponges
- contraceptive creams and jellies
- contraceptive foams
- contraceptive suppository capsules and films

Other alternatives include fertility awareness methods in concert with temporary abstinence, and withdrawal. Voluntary sterilization should be regarded as permanent because its reversal cannot be guaranteed.

Questions to be considered with all of these methods are:

- how the method works
- how dependable the method is, since only total abstinence is certain to prevent pregnancy
- advantages and disadvantages
- who can use the method
- possible problems
- cost

A variety of informative brochures that address these and other concerns are available at no cost from clinics, hospitals, and any local Planned Parenthood office.

UNPLANNED PREGNANCIES

Right now, all the foregoing thoughts, feelings, dreams, and concerns about parenting might seem like very long-range planning indeed. After all, you're still in the middle of wedding arrangements. Well, long-range planning is exactly what it is. It's taking a look down the road at creating a family and sharing with each other what's most important to both of you in that venture.

Along with the exciting possibilities, you've also considered potential difficulties, such as the inability of conceiving and bearing your own children, and raising a child who could be handicapped. A further prospect to be shared is the possibility of an unplanned pregnancy. Even in the best of all possible worlds, children aren't always planned for. And an unexpected pregnancy presents a situation that deserves some forethought. The legal alternatives, apart from any moral considerations, are:

- taking the pregnancy to term and parenting your new child;
- adoption, an alternative seldom chosen by married couples;
- terminating the pregnancy through abortion.

Each of these alternatives is value-laden. Each is emotionally charged as well. If for some reason you are not sure you wish to take the pregnancy to term or to parent the child, you will want to seek the advice and counsel of your pastor, physician, or possibly another professional counselor. Keep in mind that competent counselors will assist you in considering ethical, medical, and psychological facets of a decision that you might not otherwise see. They will not make the decision for you.

As two persons planning marriage, you likely have very strong convictions about the three legal alternatives because they involve fundamental moral issues. Therefore, it's important to share your convictions before you're confronted with the decision. You've shared so much already. Take time now to discuss the possibility of an unplanned pregnancy.

THE IMPACT OF AIDS

Since the early 1980's AIDS (acquired immune deficiency syndrome) has been a growing health threat worldwide. However, the transmission of HIV (human immunodeficiency virus), the virus which can lead to AIDS, is hard to contract if one avoids unnecessary risks. These are the primary ways the virus is transmitted:

- oral sex (semen, preseminal fluids, and vaginal fluids can carry the virus);
- intercourse (anal or vaginal) with a person who has the virus;
- sharing needles or syringes with a person who is HIV positive,
- blood transfusions before 1985.

It is also possible for an HIV-positive mother to transmit the virus to her child during pregnancy or at the time of birth. Because of the seriousness of AIDS, couples should communicate openly and honestly before engaging in unprotected sexual experiences. Talk about whether either of you has engaged in high-risk activities such as having

unprotected sex with anyone else (that is, without proper use of a condom during intercourse or a dental dam during oral sex), sharing needles when taking drugs, or if either of you has had a blood transfusion before 1985.

Any one of these experiences in the past ten years is enough to warrant a blood test for HIV since the virus can be present that long without any symptoms. Be aware that while the test is highly accurate for antibodies (substances in the blood that fight disease organisms), those antibodies can take from six weeks to three years to develop. For this reason a test at six months and again at twelve months after possible exposure is usually recommended.

The test for HIV can be done by your doctor, a blood bank, or a clinic. Ask about confidentiality before you have the test. Most people prefer that the results not become part of their medical record. You may also want to find a testing agency that provides counseling before and after the test is administered.

INTIMACY CHECKUP

As a couple preparing for a marriage, you want to share all aspects of your lives. Below is a list of areas of intimacy in which couples can grow closer together. Rate how you think you are doing in each area and prioritize what areas you believe you need to work on. Then share the results.

In the left column, prioritize the areas of intimacy in the order that you feel is most important to you personally (1 = most important, 10 = least important).

In the right column, rate how strongly you feel each area of intimacy is present in your relationship right now (1 = not present, 2 = present to a small degree, 3 = present to a considerable degree, 4 = very strongly present).

Prioritize 1–10   **Rate 1–4**

_____   **Emotional intimacy**—feeling close, able to share thoughts, hopes, and desires.   _____

_____   **Intellectual intimacy**—sharing in the world of ideas, able to talk about current affairs, literature, or any area of the human spirit.   _____

_____   **Sexual intimacy**—experiencing closeness and union through physical sharing.   _____

_____   **Recreational intimacy**—having fun together in activities of mutual interest, playing, and enjoying new adventures.   _____

_____   **Work intimacy**—sharing common tasks, such as household jobs, yardwork, community service projects; being interested in the other person's daily work.   _____

_____   **Communication intimacy**—using good communication skills in clear, honest discussions.   _____

_____   **Aesthetic intimacy**—appreciating the performing, written, and visual arts, seeing the beauty in nature and the products of human effort.   _____

_____   **Crisis intimacy**—dealing together with issues ranging from the small and everyday to the most difficult and troublesome.   _____

_____   **Commitment intimacy**—trusting each other based on faithfulness and togetherness.   _____

_____   **Conflict intimacy**—resolving differences in a constructive manner.   _____

TOWARD INTIMACY

Intimacy, that special kind of total trust and friendship that forms the heart of marriage, requires knowing the other person deeply and allowing ourselves to be fully known.

Achieving such mutual understanding requires attention, effort, time, and a little humility. Here is a "growth" barometer to help you judge whether you are moving toward intimacy.

Depending on the stage of your relationship, fill out as many of vertical boxes A through D as apply.

Under the headings I through V rank your insight from 1 to 10. Let 1 represent a minimum amount of insight and effort while 10 represents a maximum amount of effort and insight. Choose and write down, as honestly as you can, the number that would best rate your feelings at the stated times.

Compare your responses with those of your partner and explain them to each other.

	I Knowledge of myself	II Knowledge of my partner	III Willingness to allow myself to be known by my partner	IV Effort to know my partner better	V Ability to be more open to and accepting of others because of the security I have gained from our relationship
A. When we first met					
B. Going steady					
C. When engaged					
D. Today					

INTIMACY CHECKUP

As a couple preparing for a marriage, you want to share all aspects of your lives. Below is a list of areas of intimacy in which couples can grow closer together. Rate how you think you are doing in each area and prioritize what areas you believe you need to work on. Then share the results.

In the left column, prioritize the areas of intimacy in the order that you feel is most important to you personally (1 = most important, 10 = least important).

In the right column, rate how strongly you feel each area of intimacy is present in your relationship right now (1 = not present, 2 = present to a small degree, 3 = present to a considerable degree, 4 = very strongly present).

Prioritize 1–10   Rate 1–4

_____   **Emotional intimacy**—feeling close, able to share thoughts, hopes, and desires.   _____

_____   **Intellectual intimacy**—sharing in the world of ideas, able to talk about current affairs, literature, or any area of the human spirit.   _____

_____   **Sexual intimacy**—experiencing closeness and union through physical sharing.   _____

_____   **Recreational intimacy**—having fun together in activities of mutual interest, playing, and enjoying new adventures.   _____

_____   **Work intimacy**—sharing common tasks, such as household jobs, yardwork, community service projects; being interested in the other person's daily work.   _____

_____   **Communication intimacy**—using good communication skills in clear, honest discussions.   _____

_____   **Aesthetic intimacy**—appreciating the performing, written, and visual arts, seeing the beauty in nature and the products of human effort.   _____

_____   **Crisis intimacy**—dealing together with issues ranging from the small and everyday to the most difficult and troublesome.   _____

_____   **Commitment intimacy**—trusting each other based on faithfulness and togetherness.   _____

_____   **Conflict intimacy**—resolving differences in a constructive manner.   _____

TOWARD INTIMACY

Intimacy, that special kind of total trust and friendship that forms the heart of marriage, requires knowing the other person deeply and allowing ourselves to be fully known.

Achieving such mutual understanding requires attention, effort, time, and a little humility. Here is a "growth" barometer to help you judge whether you are moving toward intimacy.

Depending on the stage of your relationship, fill out as many of vertical boxes A through D as apply.

Under the headings I through V rank your insight from 1 to 10. Let 1 represent a minimum amount of insight and effort while 10 represents a maximum amount of effort and insight. Choose and write down, as honestly as you can, the number that would best rate your feelings at the stated times.

Compare your responses with those of your partner and explain them to each other.

	I Knowledge of myself	II Knowledge of my partner	III Willingness to allow myself to be known by my partner	IV Effort to know my partner better	V Ability to be more open to and accepting of others because of the security I have gained from our relationship
A. When we first met					
B. Going steady					
C. When engaged					
D. Today					

IF WE DON'T KNOW WHERE WE COME FROM

Your family of origin is the family in which each of you had your beginnings—physically, spiritually, psychologically, and emotionally. It is the family in which you were raised. The impact of your family of origin on each of you is deep and pervasive and will continue to influence you throughout your entire lifetime.

This exercise will help you identify the ways of relating inside your families of origin that helped each of you become the person you are today.

Answer each of the questions below about the family in which you were raised. Circle one, and only one, of the five dots on each horizontal line

under the category that best describes your view of how your family of origin operated. Your choices are: ALWAYS, USUALLY, SOMETIMES, SELDOM, NEVER.

When you have finished, compare your results with your partner and discuss the areas in which you had definite differences in family experience. Decide how you would like your new family to function. If you cannot agree now, set time aside to discuss the issue at greater length. It is important for the two of you to agree on a plan to resolve differences in relating that will be workable after you are married.

ALWAYS	USUALLY	SOMETIMES	SELDOM	NEVER	
•	•	•	•	•	Did your family encourage you to express what you thought?
•	•	•	•	•	Did your family encourage you to express how you felt?
•	•	•	•	•	In your family, did people take responsibility for their actions?
•	•	•	•	•	Did your family encourage the expression of differences of opinions?
•	•	•	•	•	Were members of your family encouraged to listen closely to each other?
•	•	•	•	•	Did your family express their emotions openly about death, divorce, or other painful losses?
•	•	•	•	•	Was it acceptable in your family to express both positive and negative feelings?

ALWAYS	USUALLY	SOMETIMES	SELDOM	NEVER	
•	•	•	•	•	Was your family supportive when you tried "new things"?
•	•	•	•	•	Were you able to work out conflicts in your family?
•	•	•	•	•	Did your family allow anger to be expressed constructively?
•	•	•	•	•	Did your family exhibit a sense of humor?
•	•	•	•	•	Was your family sensitive to one another's feelings?
•	•	•	•	•	Did your family encourage you to trust others?
•	•	•	•	•	Did your family tolerate abusive behavior (verbal, physical, sexual)?
•	•	•	•	•	Did your family relate to each other with both physical and verbal expressions of affection?

Your reactions to the relationships inside your individual families of origin will, in many ways, determine how the family you are starting together will operate. Your families of origin will naturally involve themselves in your relationship. How you handle that involvement will go a long way toward

shaping your marriage and family. You may also be faced at some point in your marriage with caring for an aged or ill parent or other relative. Now is the time to begin to discuss how you will respond to that need.

MY FAMILY, YOUR FAMILY, OUR FAMILY

This exercise is designed to surface anxiety you might have about the involvement of your families in your marriage. The following statements will help you clarify both your understanding of situations and your concerns about them. They will also clarify any misunderstandings you might have about your partner's reactions to either family.

Remember: there is often a big difference between how you or your partner *think* (rationally, intellectually) about something and whether or not you are *bothered* (emotionally, on a feeling basis) about it. You may *think* something is true and yet not be *bothered* (apprehensive, nervous, worried, uptight) about it, or you may *feel* concerned about something even if you have no evidence that it is true.

First, mark the left side of the list under each category—(A) I THINK, (B) BOTHERS ME—with your own reactions. Circle one dot for each statement under each column. Remember: the first column is what you *think* to be the case, the second column is how you truly *feel* about the situation.

When you have finished the entire list regarding your own reactions, go back and *re-read* each statement from what you believe is your partner's point of view. Then mark the right side of the list under each category—(C) YOU THINK, (D) BOTHERS YOU—with how you believe your partner will respond. Circle one dot for each statement under each column.

(A) I THINK	(B) BOTHERS ME		(C) I THINK	(D) BOTHERS ME
YES NO NOT SURE	YES NO NOT SURE		YES NO NOT SURE	YES NO NOT SURE
• • •	• • •	1. One or both of our families of origin do not support our decision to marry.	• • •	• • •
• • •	• • •	2. Your family does not accept me.	• • •	• • •
• • •	• • •	3. My family does not accept you.	• • •	• • •
• • •	• • •	4. We will have difficulties in our marriage because our families of origin are of significantly different social, religious, or economic backgrounds.	• • •	• • •
• • •	• • •	5. One or both of our families of origin will interfere in our marital relationship.	• • •	• • •
• • •	• • •	6. One or both of our families of origin will interfere in our decisions on running our household or raising our children.	• • •	• • •
• • •	• • •	7. One or both of us is unwilling to discuss our role in caring for our parents or other relatives in their old age or illness.	• • •	• • •
• • •	• • •	8. Our own family will be affected by our having to care for one or more of our parents or other relatives in their old age or illness.	• • •	• • •

Compare the answers each of you gave for A and B with those your partner gave for C and D.

If you differ on your perception of your relationships with your two families of origin (what you think is the situation), you need to discuss these items openly and honestly and decide how you are going to determine what is truly the case.

If one of you has a definite concern on a specific issue or if you gave different answers regarding one another's concerns (what you *feel* about the situation), it means that there are anxieties that still exist regarding your families of origin with which you must still deal.

IF WE DON'T KNOW WHERE WE COME FROM

Your family of origin is the family in which each of you had your beginnings—physically, spiritually, psychologically, and emotionally. It is the family in which you were raised. The impact of your family of origin on each of you is deep and pervasive and will continue to influence you throughout your entire lifetime.

This exercise will help you identify the ways of relating inside your families of origin that helped each of you become the person you are today.

Answer each of the questions below about the family in which you were raised. Circle one, and only one, of the five dots on each horizontal line under the category that best describes your view of how your family of origin operated. Your choices are: ALWAYS, USUALLY, SOMETIMES, SELDOM, NEVER.

When you have finished, compare your results with your partner and discuss the areas in which you had definite differences in family experience. Decide how you would like your new family to function. If you cannot agree now, set time aside to discuss the issue at greater length. It is important for the two of you to agree on a plan to resolve differences in relating that will be workable after you are married.

ALWAYS	USUALLY	SOMETIMES	SELDOM	NEVER	
•	•	•	•	•	Did your family encourage you to express what you thought?
•	•	•	•	•	Did your family encourage you to express how you felt?
•	•	•	•	•	In your family, did people take responsibility for their actions?
•	•	•	•	•	Did your family encourage the expression of differences of opinions?
•	•	•	•	•	Were members of your family encouraged to listen closely to each other?
•	•	•	•	•	Did your family express their emotions openly about death, divorce, or other painful losses?
•	•	•	•	•	Was it acceptable in your family to express both positive and negative feelings?

ALWAYS	USUALLY	SOMETIMES	SELDOM	NEVER	
•	•	•	•	•	Was your family supportive when you tried "new things"?
•	•	•	•	•	Were you able to work out conflicts in your family?
•	•	•	•	•	Did your family allow anger to be expressed constructively?
•	•	•	•	•	Did your family exhibit a sense of humor?
•	•	•	•	•	Was your family sensitive to one another's feelings?
•	•	•	•	•	Did your family encourage you to trust others?
•	•	•	•	•	Did your family tolerate abusive behavior (verbal, physical, sexual)?
•	•	•	•	•	Did your family relate to each other with both physical and verbal expressions of affection?

Your reactions to the relationships inside your individual families of origin will, in many ways, determine how the family you are starting together will operate. Your families of origin will naturally involve themselves in your relationship. How you handle that involvement will go a long way toward shaping your marriage and family. You may also be faced at some point in your marriage with caring for an aged or ill parent or other relative. Now is the time to begin to discuss how you will respond to that need.

MY FAMILY, YOUR FAMILY, OUR FAMILY

This exercise is designed to surface anxiety you might have about the involvement of your families in your marriage. The following statements will help you clarify both your understanding of situations and your concerns about them. They will also clarify any misunderstandings you might have about your partner's reactions to either family.

Remember: there is often a big difference between how you or your partner *think* (rationally, intellectually) about something and whether or not you are *bothered* (emotionally, on a feeling basis) about it. You may *think* something is true and yet not be *bothered* (apprehensive, nervous, worried, uptight) about it, or you may *feel* concerned about something even if you have no evidence that it is true.

First, mark the left side of the list under each category—(A) I THINK, (B) BOTHERS ME—with your own reactions. Circle one dot for each statement under each column. Remember: the first column is what you *think* to be the case, the second column is how you truly *feel* about the situation.

When you have finished the entire list regarding your own reactions, go back and *re-read* each statement from what you believe is your partner's point of view. Then mark the right side of the list under each category—(C) YOU THINK, (D) BOTHERS YOU—with how you believe your partner will respond. Circle one dot for each statement under each column.

(A) I THINK	(B) BOTHERS ME		(C) I THINK	(D) BOTHERS ME
YES NO NOT SURE	YES NO NOT SURE		YES NO NOT SURE	YES NO NOT SURE
• • •	• • •	1. One or both of our families of origin do not support our decision to marry.	• • •	• • •
• • •	• • •	2. Your family does not accept me.	• • •	• • •
• • •	• • •	3. My family does not accept you.	• • •	• • •
• • •	• • •	4. We will have difficulties in our marriage because our families of origin are of significantly different social, religious, or economic backgrounds.	• • •	• • •
• • •	• • •	5. One or both of our families of origin will interfere in our marital relationship.	• • •	• • •
• • •	• • •	6. One or both of our families of origin will interfere in our decisions on running our household or raising our children.	• • •	• • •
• • •	• • •	7. One or both of us is unwilling to discuss our role in caring for our parents or other relatives in their old age or illness.	• • •	• • •
• • •	• • •	8. Our own family will be affected by our having to care for one or more of our parents or other relatives in their old age or illness.	• • •	• • •

Compare the answers each of you gave for A and B with those your partner gave for C and D.

If you differ on your perception of your relationships with your two families of origin (what you think is the situation), you need to discuss these items openly and honestly and decide how you are going to determine what is truly the case.

If one of you has a definite concern on a specific issue or if you gave different answers regarding one another's concerns (what you *feel* about the situation), it means that there are anxieties that still exist regarding your families of origin with which you must still deal.

NOW'S THE TIME

One of the most important tasks facing your relationship is creating a new family. Today, it is possible to prevent or encourage conception of babies safely and naturally. Medical progress has also meant that babies with handicaps now survive more readily. You might be called to raise a handicapped child yourselves. There is also a need for more adoptive and foster homes for children with special needs. That too may be part of the gift of your marriage. It is your responsibility as a married couple to decide the nature of your own family in light of the Christian faith, the teachings of your church, and your personal ethics.

Problems in marriage arise as often from misunderstandings as from differences of opinion. This is never more true than over issues involving children. The following is a quick and easy exercise to confirm that you both have the same understandings about having and raising children, even though these understandings will certainly grow and mature over the years. On issues like these, don't assume that you have reached accord unless you have specifically done so.

For each issue, answer these two questions:

- Have you discussed this matter to your satisfaction?
- Have you agreed upon an answer for the time being?

Circle one dot for each issue under each column.

Have we discussed?				Have we agreed upon?		
YES	NO	NOT SURE		YES	NO	NOT SURE
•	•	•	Having children?	•	•	•
•	•	•	Whether we are prepared to be parents?	•	•	•
•	•	•	The number of children we want?	•	•	•
•	•	•	How we will attempt to space our children's births?	•	•	•
•	•	•	What method(s) of birth control will we use?	•	•	•
•	•	•	When we would like to begin having children?	•	•	•
•	•	•	Not being able to have children of our own?	•	•	•
•	•	•	The possibility of adopting or fostering children?	•	•	•
•	•	•	The possibility of raising a handicapped child?	•	•	•
•	•	•	Our beliefs about the way to discipline children?	•	•	•
•	•	•	The future education of our children?	•	•	•
•	•	•	The religious upbringing of our children?	•	•	•

Now compare your responses. Where there is disagreement or where either of you have answered "Not Sure," there is need for further discussion both before and after the wedding. These questions are too important to ignore. You might want to save this exercise and redo it each year on your anniversary, just to make sure you're both on the same wavelength regarding the development of your family.

ARE WE READY?

The questions raised in this exercise are designed to help you begin to think about how prepared you are to assume the vocation of father and mother.

Working alone, complete each of the following statements about your future family. Try to use phrases or sentences in your responses.

Share the results with your partner and then discuss your answers. Focus on those issues about which you have important concerns or differences and discuss how you will resolve them.

Three important qualities I think I will have as a parent:

_____

_____

My greatest concern about my ability to be a good parent:

_____

_____

Three important qualities I think you will have as a parent:

_____

_____

My greatest concern about your ability to be a good parent:

_____

_____

The main attitudes and behaviors I want to cultivate in our children:

_____

_____

How we can prepare ourselves for parenthood:

_____

_____

Some of the best role models I have known for parenting:

_____

_____

Resources we can turn to for help in parenting:

_____

_____

NOW'S THE TIME

One of the most important tasks facing your relationship is creating a new family. Today, it is possible to prevent or encourage conception of babies safely and naturally. Medical progress has also meant that babies with handicaps now survive more readily. You might be called to raise a handicapped child yourselves. There is also a need for more adoptive and foster homes for children with special needs. That too may be part of the gift of your marriage. It is your responsibility as a married couple to decide the nature of your own family in light of the Christian faith, the teachings of your church, and your personal ethics.

Problems in marriage arise as often from misunderstandings as from differences of opinion. This is never more true than over issues involving children. The following is a quick and easy exercise to confirm that you both have the same understandings about having and raising children, even though these understandings will certainly grow and mature over the years. On issues like these, don't assume that you have reached accord unless you have specifically done so.

For each issue, answer these two questions:

* Have you discussed this matter to your satisfaction?

* Have you agreed upon an answer for the time being?

Circle one dot for each issue under each column.

Have we discussed?				Have we agreed upon?		
YES	NO	NOT SURE		YES	NO	NOT SURE
•	•	•	Having children?	•	•	•
•	•	•	Whether we are prepared to be parents?	•	•	•
•	•	•	The number of children we want?	•	•	•
•	•	•	How we will attempt to space our children's births?	•	•	•
•	•	•	What method(s) of birth control will we use?	•	•	•
•	•	•	When we would like to begin having children?	•	•	•
•	•	•	Not being able to have children of our own?	•	•	•
•	•	•	The possibility of adopting or fostering children?	•	•	•
•	•	•	The possibility of raising a handicapped child?	•	•	•
•	•	•	Our beliefs about the way to discipline children?	•	•	•
•	•	•	The future education of our children?	•	•	•
•	•	•	The religious upbringing of our children?	•	•	•

Now compare your responses. Where there is disagreement or where either of you have answered "Not Sure," there is need for further discussion both before and after the wedding. These questions are too important to ignore. You might want to save this exercise and redo it each year on your anniversary, just to make sure you're both on the same wavelength regarding the development of your family.

ARE WE READY?

The questions raised in this exercise are designed to help you begin to think about how prepared you are to assume the vocation of father and mother.

Working alone, complete each of the following statements about your future family. Write or print the answers clearly so your partner can read them. Try to use phrases or sentences in your responses.

Share the results with your partner and then discuss your answers. Focus on those issues about which you have important concerns or differences and discuss how you will resolve them.

Three important qualities I think I will have as a parent:

_____

_____

My greatest concern about my ability to be a good parent:

_____

_____

Three important qualities I think you will have as a parent:

_____

_____

My greatest concern about your ability to be a good parent:

_____

_____

The main attitudes and behaviors I want to cultivate in our children:

_____

_____

How we can prepare ourselves for parenthood:

_____

_____

Some of the best role models I have known for parenting:

_____

_____

Resources we can turn to for help in parenting:

_____

_____

ALCOHOL AND DRUG ABUSE WITHIN MARRIAGE

You've been together for a while now and know that being in love is wonderful. You're healthy and happy, and you have fun together. In our society, having fun often includes using some alcohol or drugs. Maybe one or both of you "party" a little too much from time to time. Or, when the pressure's on, you may use uppers or downers to smooth things out—diet pills, sleeping pills, tranquilizers, or any of the other mood- or mind-altering chemicals that are so available today.

Occasional alcohol or drug use doesn't mean you're an alcoholic or an addict. But it *does* mean that you face the possibility of having your occasional *use* of alcohol or drugs turn into a serious *abuse* problem.

While you may not want to think about chemical abuse during this happy time in your relationship, you can't afford to ignore the facts. Alcohol and drug dependency is now one of our nation's most serious health problems. Only cancer and heart disease cause more deaths. Dependency on mood-altering chemicals including alcohol is a factor in 80 percent of all suicides, 64 percent of all auto fatalities, and nearly two-thirds of the reported incidents of physical abuse. One out of every four families in the United States is affected by chemical abuse.

Chemical dependency is considered a disease by the health care professions. But no one wants to admit being an alcoholic or an addict. People who pass from casual alcohol and drug use to abuse will drink and use drugs in ever-increasing amounts as their disease progresses, while denying the changes that are taking place in their lives. Their behavior becomes increasingly unpredictable. Their personalities begin to change for the worse. Their work performance, social life, health, and family relationships suffer. When pressured to control themselves, they minimize the problem, get angry, or withdraw. Even sheer willpower won't stop them from using again.

Helping chemical dependency to remain the great hidden disease are the enablers—those family members and loved ones who will not face the fact that the one they love is an alcoholic or an addict. They avoid talking to the abuser about the problem because they don't want to upset him or her. They allow abusers to continue their sick behavior by covering for them and bailing them out when they get into trouble. Only when pushed to the wall—when they cannot hide the facts from outsiders, or when the abuser becomes physically abusive as well—will many families seek help for their loved ones, or for themselves.

You don't want this kind of a scenario in your marriage, for yourself, your partner, or your children. So what can you do?

First, answer the questions on the following pages to evaluate your own situation.

Next, discuss your answers honestly and openly. Talk about your attitudes and feelings. Try not to minimize a problem, hide anything from your partner, or hold back honest feelings. This is one area where your love alone will not see you through. If there is a possibility of a problem existing now, the added pressures of marriage and family life will only worsen the situation.

Finally, if you have any unanswered questions, or if you suspect that a problem may exist, contact a professional. Chemical dependency, like any other serious illness, should be diagnosed and treated by professionals. In this field there are many specialists, both in the health care field and in self-help groups. For help, or more information, contact the local offices of Alcoholics Anonymous, Narcotics Anonymous, Al-Anon, or the family services or mental health services of your church body. Many hospitals now are providing counseling and treatment. If none of these organizations exist in your community, you can contact the following national offices for referrals to both public and private services.

Al-Anon Family Group Headquarters
1372 Broadway
New York, NY 10018-0862

Alateen
1372 Broadway
New York, NY 10018-0862

Alcoholics Anonymous
General Service Office
P.O. Box 459
Grand Central Station
New York, NY 10163

Narcotics Anonymous
World Service Office, Inc.
P.O. Box 999
Van Nuys, CA 91409

National Association for Children of Alcoholics, Inc.
31582 Coast Highway
Suite B
South Laguna, CA 92677-3044

National Clearinghouse for Alcohol/Drug Information
P.O. Box 2345
Rockville, MD 20852

National Coalition Against Domestic Violence (NCADV)
1500 Massachusetts Ave. NW
Washington, D.C. 20005

TOUGH QUESTIONS ABOUT ALCOHOL AND DRUGS

Working alone, place a check mark in the appropriate column if the statement is even slightly true for yourself or—to the best of your knowledge—for your future spouse. If you are unsure of your response to any question, put a question mark in the appropriate column. When you are finished, share your responses with each other. If either of you (or both) have several check or question marks, you should definitely discuss your concerns with each other, seek more information, and get some help before the wedding.

TRUE FOR ME   **TRUE FOR MY PARTNER**

1. Do either of you lose time from work because of drinking or using drugs?

2. Is drinking or drug use making either of your lives unhappy in any way?

3. Do either of you drink or use drugs because you are shy or uncomfortable around other people?

4. Is drinking or drug use affecting either of your reputations?

5. Have either of you gotten into financial difficulties as a result of drinking or using drugs?

6. Do either of you turn to different companions or an inappropriate environment when drinking or using drugs?

7. Do either of you need to get "high" at a definite time each day or week?

8. Do either of you want a "chaser" the next morning after partying?

9. Has alcohol or drugs ever caused either of you to have difficulty sleeping?

10. Do either of you drink or take drugs to escape from worries or trouble?

11. Do either of you drink or take drugs to build up your self-confidence?

12. Have either of you ever been concerned about your own or your partner's drinking or use of drugs?

13. Have either of you ever extracted promises about drinking or drug use from the other that were not kept?

14. Have either of you made threats or decisions because of the other's use of alcohol or drugs?

15. Do either of you feel responsible for or guilty about the other's use of alcohol or drugs?

16. Do either of you try to conceal your own or the other's drinking or use of drugs, or deny there is a problem despite strong evidence of its existence?

17. Have either of you ever avoided activities with families and friends because of fear of embarrassment over the other's use of alcohol or drugs?

18. Have either of you ever felt the need to justify to someone else your own, or your partner's, attitude toward or use of alcohol or drugs?

19. Do either of you exhibit any physical symptoms such as nausea, a "knot" in the stomach, ulcers, shakiness, sweating palms, bitten fingernails because of your own or your partner's drinking or use of drugs?

20. Do either of you feel helpless about your own or your partner's use of alcohol or drugs—that nothing you or anyone else can do will make the situation better?

A NOTE ON PHYSICAL ABUSE WITHIN MARRIAGE

One of the by-products of alcohol and drug abuse is often physical abuse. Physical abuse is something we sometimes joke about ("To the moon, Alice . . ."), but it is more serious and widespread than many realize. Physical abuse happens among all classes and races, regardless of their income and educational levels. Violence in the home usually becomes more frequent and serious over time, often fueled by alcohol or drugs. It is part of an escalating pattern that begins with threats, insults, jealousy, explosive tempers, and attempts to isolate or overpower the other.

Children from violent homes learn to regard violence as an acceptable means of control and a normal way of responding to disappointment and frustration. When they grow up, these children are very likely to become abusers themselves.

Like alcohol and drug abuse, physical abuse needs to be dealt with if it is part of your relationship. If you need help, get it now—before the wedding. The one thing that is sure is that the problem will not go away after you are married.

TOUGH QUESTIONS ABOUT ALCOHOL AND DRUGS

Working alone, place a check mark in the appropriate column if the statement is even slightly true for yourself or—to the best of your knowledge—for your future spouse. If you are unsure of your response to any question, put a question mark in the appropriate column. When you are finished, share your responses with each other. If either of you (or both) have several check or question marks, you should definitely discuss your concerns with each other, seek more information, and get some help before the wedding.

TRUE FOR ME   **TRUE FOR MY PARTNER**

1. Do either of you lose time from work because of drinking or using drugs?

2. Is drinking or drug use making either of your lives unhappy in any way?

3. Do either of you drink or use drugs because you are shy or uncomfortable around other people?

4. Is drinking or drug use affecting either of your reputations?

5. Have either of you gotten into financial difficulties as a result of drinking or using drugs?

6. Do either of you turn to different companions or an inappropriate environment when drinking or using drugs?

7. Do either of you need to get "high" at a definite time each day or week?

8. Do either of you want a "chaser" the next morning after partying?

9. Has alcohol or drugs ever caused either of you to have difficulty sleeping?

10. Do either of you drink or take drugs to escape from worries or trouble?

11. Do either of you drink or take drugs to build up your self-confidence?

12. Have either of you ever been concerned about your own or your partner's drinking or use of drugs?

13. Have either of you ever extracted promises about drinking or drug use from the other that were not kept?

14. Have either of you made threats or decisions because of the other's use of alcohol or drugs?

15. Do either of you feel responsible for or guilty about the other's use of alcohol or drugs?

16. Do either of you try to conceal your own or the other's drinking or use of drugs, or deny there is a problem despite strong evidence of its existence?

17. Have either of you ever avoided activities with families and friends because of fear of embarrassment over the other's use of alcohol or drugs?

18. Have either of you ever felt the need to justify to someone else your own, or your partner's, attitude toward or use of alcohol or drugs?

19. Do either of you exhibit any physical symptoms such as nausea, a "knot" in the stomach, ulcers, shakiness, sweating palms, bitten fingernails because of your own or your partner's drinking or use of drugs?

20. Do either of you feel helpless about your own or your partner's use of alcohol or drugs—that nothing you or anyone else can do will make the situation better?

A NOTE ON PHYSICAL ABUSE WITHIN MARRIAGE

One of the by-products of alcohol and drug abuse is often physical abuse. Physical abuse is something we sometimes joke about ("To the moon, Alice . . ."), but it is more serious and widespread than many realize. Physical abuse happens among all classes and races, regardless of their income and educational levels. Violence in the home usually becomes more frequent and serious over time, often fueled by alcohol or drugs. It is part of an escalating pattern that begins with threats, insults, jealousy, explosive tempers, and attempts to isolate or overpower the other.

Children from violent homes learn to regard violence as an acceptable means of control and a normal way of responding to disappointment and frustration. When they grow up, these children are very likely to become abusers themselves.

Like alcohol and drug abuse, physical abuse needs to be dealt with if it is part of your relationship. If you need help, get it now—before the wedding. The one thing that is sure is that the problem will not go away after you are married.

THE DOLLAR ALMIGHTY?

Like the flag, the cross, or a kiss, money is a powerful symbol. Having it can mean security, status, comfort, freedom, control, acceptance. The lack of it can mean fear, depression, inferiority, guilt, anxiety.

Discuss the following questions together:

- What are your individual attitudes on money?

- How has your experience in your own families of origin formed your individual attitudes?

- How will money matters be handled in your marriage? (Who will keep the checkbook? Pay the bills? Do the banking? Make investment decisions?)

- How are you going to communicate about money? When crises arise? At set intervals (daily, weekly, monthly, yearly)?

- Will you share your money with others? How? How much? When?

TWO INCOMES

Most couples getting married today have two incomes. You need to discuss if this will always be the case in your marriage. Might you decide to go to a single income when children arrive or in order for one of you to attend school or for some other reason? If so, then you need to plan for that change now. Will you enjoy the benefits of two incomes on a short-term basis or will you save the "extra" money you earn now for later?

THREE COUPLES TO PITY

Couple #1: Believe time is money. They know the price of everything but the value of nothing. They would sell their souls for the right price. They are dead in spirit years before they have the good grace to lie down.

Couple #2: Believe the world owes them a living. They seem to despise work and have no realization that humans are called to contribute to the ongoing creation of the universe. They are parasites—sometimes attractive, intelligent, or highly entertaining—but parasites nonetheless.

Couple #3: Have good intentions but are undisciplined and unreflective. They fall prey to every desire excited in them by advertisers and the media. They overstretch their credit, overestimate their earnings, underestimate their bills, and never dream of planning or budgeting.

POSSESS OR BE POSSESSED

You can be possessed by the things you possess. They can claim your time and effort in paying for them, as well as sap your emotional and physical energy worrying about them, protecting them, caring for them. They can fill your imagination with dreams of how to get more of them.

The first fruit of true freedom is poverty
　of spirit,
of detachment,
of schooling yourself in not wanting
　everything.

If you are truly in love, your love for each other will want to burst out of your relationship—like new wine in old wineskins. You will want to give, not take. The best gift you can give is yourselves—your time, your interest, your talents—to projects, to works of compassion, to worthy causes. Nor can you ignore your treasure (however meager it may be at the moment)! If you are truly thankful for the blessing of your love, you will want to share your possessions with those less fortunate than you.

Give as if your marriage depended on it. It does.

YOUR FIRST-YEAR BUDGET

| | ESTIMATED BUDGET | ACTUAL DOLLARS SPENT |

MONTHS

INCOME	1	2	3	4	5	6	7	8	9	10	11	12	TOTAL
Salary(ies)													
Bonus(es)													
Dividends													
Interest													
Tax Returns													
Sales of assets													
Other													
Total Estimated Income													
Total Actual Income													

MONTHS

EXPENSES	1	2	3	4	5	6	7	8	9	10	11	12	TOTAL
HOUSING Mortgage/Rent													
Taxes													
Insurance													
Utilities													
Maintenance													
Improvements													
TRANSPORTATION Car Payments													
Insurance													
Gas & Oil													
Parking													
License/Permits													
Commuting													

Directions: Fill in your expense and income projections in the unshaded areas. As your year progresses, fill in the actual dollars spent and earned in the shaded areas. Compare those figures in the shaded areas to those in the unshaded areas to evaluate your budgeting. At the end subtract expenses from income as a final measure of your financial situation.

Note: We've numbered the months rather than naming them as this is supposed to be a budget for your first year of marriage. You can start either with January or with your first month of marriage, whichever makes the most sense to you.

ESTIMATED BUDGET | **ACTUAL DOLLARS SPENT**

	EXPENSES	1	2	3	4	5	6	7	8	9	10	11	12	TOTAL
FOOD	Groceries													
	Restaurants													
CLOTHING	Purchases													
	Cleaning													
HEALTH CARE	Medical/Dental													
	Drugs/Medicine													
	Insurance													
RECREATION	Entertainment													
	Vacations													
	Hobbies													
	Gifts													
	Contributions													
	Life Insurance													
	Installment Payments													
	Savings													
	Personal Allow. HERS													
	Personal Allow. HIS													
	Miscellaneous													
	Total estimated expenses													
	Total actual expenses													

Actual Income $ _____

LESS Actual Expenses _____

Final Total $ _____

Estimated Income $ _____

LESS Estimated Expenses _____

Final Total $ _____

FINANCIAL PLANNING

As a means of coordinating resources and expenditures, a budget is a financial plan. Just as stockholders in a business insist on intelligent financial planning from the managers of the business, marriage partners must cooperate with one another to manage income sensibly and ensure their financial security.

Adopt a budget to suit your special circumstances as a couple. Consider the questions listed below, and use the sample budget as a guide when developing your financial plan.

Which of you will have primary responsibility for maintaining the budget?

Who is better qualified?

Should both partners alternate responsibility?

Should responsibility be shared equally?

Should only one partner be responsible?

The two-income family creates a new set of alternatives, requiring more careful management of both financial and emotional resources.

Have you agreed to plan carefully and save money, if possible?

Or, have you elected to enjoy the benefits of two incomes, perhaps on a short-term basis—at the possible price of a more uncertain financial future?

Have you identified short-term goals, such as saving for emergencies or unemployment?

Have you identified long-term goals, such as educating your children or purchasing real estate?

Have you considered the impact of inflation on your budget?

Inflation is, and will continue to be, a fact of life with which all of us must come to terms. You must be aware of rising costs, plan carefully, educate yourselves to make intelligent choices, and avoid skillful advertising ploys that encourage "buying now" before prices go even higher.

Intelligent planning, open communication, and willing cooperation will have a positive impact on your life-style and on financial security now and in the future.

TRUTHS ABOUT BUDGETS

A well-planned and well-executed budget is not a rigid set of rules, guidelines that help avoid unhappy arguments over money in marriage.

A well-planned and well-executed budget can help free you from worries over money.

The budgeting process need not be complicated. Simple arithmetic is all you need, keeping in mind that:

The money you earn is what you have to spend; the money you spend is subtracted, and that's it.

KNOWING THE TERRITORY

It is important for couples entering marriage to be totally aware of each other's present financial situation *before* making their financial arrangements as a couple. The wisest course is for each of you to lay out your financial picture as completely as possible before the wedding. Be as honest as you can—this is no time for hiding the "bad news." Don't forget to include all possible liabilities, assets, and income. After you have completed this exercise separately, exchange your sheets and discuss your financial situation openly and realistically.

YOUR LIABILITIES

	Monthly Payments (if applicable)	Total Still Owed (if applicable)	Payoff Date (if applicable)
Mortgage/Rent (including property taxes)	$	$	$
Car Loan	$	$	$
Other Installment Loans	$	$	$
Lines of Credit	$	$	$
Credit Cards	$	$	$
Other Loans	$	$	$
Personal	$	$	$
College	$	$	$
Business	$	$	$
Insurance	$	$	$
Car	$	$	$
Life	$	$	$
Home	$	$	$
Health/Disability (if not withheld)	$	$	$
Income Taxes (if not withheld)	$	$	$
Back Taxes Owed	$	$	$
Medical and Dental Bills	$	$	$
Pension/Retirement Contribution (if not withheld)	$	$	$
(If applicable):			
Child Care	$	$	$
Tuition/College Savings	$	$	$
Child Support	$	$	$
Alimony to Former Spouse	$	$	$

YOUR ASSETS
Present Estimated Value

Real Estate $ _____

Cash Savings $ _____

Certificates of Deposit $ _____

Stocks and Bonds $ _____

Pension/Retirement Accounts $ _____

Cash Value Life Insurance $ _____

Other Investments $ _____

Cars $ _____

Furniture, Artwork, Jewelry $ _____

Expected Inheritance $ _____

Other Assets $ _____

_____

YOUR INCOME
Estimated Monthly Income

Salary (Take Home) $ _____

Bonus $ _____

Dividends and Interest $ _____

Rental Income $ _____

Trusts and Gifts $ _____

Alimony (if applicable) $ _____

Child Support (if applicable) $ _____

Other Income $ _____

A Clear Picture

If you've both been able to fill in most of the information requested, you should have a good view of your financial situation as you enter your marriage. Now discuss what this means:

- Will there be enough money to cover your combined liabilities?

- How can you best combine your assets?
- What debts can be eliminated prior to the wedding?
- How much will you be able to save from your combined incomes?
- Will obligations you bring with you into marriage be able to be met?

Preparing for Marriage Copyright © 1992 Augsburg Fortress. This worksheet may be reproduced for personal use.

KNOWING THE TERRITORY

It is important for couples entering marriage to be totally aware of each other's present financial situation *before* making their financial arrangements as a couple. The wisest course is for each of you to lay out your financial picture as completely as possible before the wedding. Be as honest as you can—this is no time for hiding the "bad news." Don't forget to include all possible liabilities, assets, and income. After you have completed this exercise separately, exchange your sheets and discuss your financial situation openly and realistically.

YOUR LIABILITIES

	Monthly Payments (if applicable)	Total Still Owed (if applicable)	Payoff Date (if applicable)
Mortgage/Rent (including property taxes)	$	$	$
Car Loan	$	$	$
Other Installment Loans	$	$	$
Lines of Credit	$	$	$
Credit Cards	$	$	$
Other Loans	$	$	$
Personal	$	$	$
College	$	$	$
Business	$	$	$
Insurance			
Car	$	$	$
Life	$	$	$
Home	$	$	$
Health/Disability (if not withheld)	$	$	$
Income Taxes (if not withheld)	$	$	$
Back Taxes Owed	$	$	$
Medical and Dental Bills	$	$	$
Pension/Retirement Contribution (if not withheld)	$	$	$
(If applicable):			
Child Care	$	$	$
Tuition/College Savings	$	$	$
Child Support	$	$	$
Alimony to Former Spouse	$	$	$

YOUR ASSETS

Present Estimated Value

Real Estate	$
Cash Savings	$
Certificates of Deposit	$
Stocks and Bonds	$
Pension/Retirement Accounts	$
Cash Value Life Insurance	$
Other Investments	$
Cars	$
Furniture, Artwork, Jewelry	$
Expected Inheritance	$
Other Assets	$

YOUR INCOME

Estimated Monthly Income

Salary (Take Home)	$
Bonus	$
Dividends and Interest	$
Rental Income	$
Trusts and Gifts	$
Alimony (if applicable)	$
Child Support (if applicable)	$
Other Income	$

A Clear Picture

If you've both been able to fill in most of the information requested, you should have a good view of your financial situation as you enter your marriage. Now discuss what this means:

- Will there be enough money to cover your combined liabilities?

- How can you best combine your assets?
- What debts can be eliminated prior to the wedding?
- How much will you be able to save from your combined incomes?
- Will obligations you bring with you into marriage be able to be met?

GETTING YOUR NEW FINANCIAL HOUSE IN ORDER

"**A** loaf of bread, a jug of wine, and thou beside me singing in the wilderness, and wilderness were paradise enough!"

This famous line from *The Rubaiyat* is used at many weddings. It sums up beautifully the feeling couples have that all they need is each other to be happy. Ask any married couple, however, and they will tell you that it is also important to learn about such mundane things as money management and budgeting if a marriage is going to succeed. Here are some money matters that you need to consider as you begin your marriage:

1. **Credit.** A good credit rating is a necessity in this world. Without it you cannot cash a check, buy a house, or even rent a car. To establish a good credit rating you must have a record of faithful, regular repayment of debt. Couples can begin to establish a combined credit rating by opening joint checking and savings accounts and by obtaining one of the many credit cards now available. The important thing in establishing credit is to pay your bills promptly and not to run up huge debts that you have no ability to repay. It is also important that you each maintain your individual credit rating. Thus, it might be helpful for each of you to have at least one credit card in your own name that you use occasionally and pay off immediately.

2. **Debt.** Many couples find that they can obtain credit easily—sometimes credit cards even come unsolicited through the mail! In the first few years of marriage, especially if they have two incomes, couples often find it tempting to purchase items on credit, enjoy them immediately, and pay for them later. If they accumulate too large a debt, however, couples can find themselves in serious financial trouble. If unexpected expenses occur, if one or both lose their jobs, if children arrive, the couple can quickly find themselves owing more money than they can repay. Sometimes they cannot even keep up the interest payments. If you find yourself in this situation, seek immediate financial counseling. An advisor can help you deal with creditors and arrange a repayment schedule that will allow you to maintain a good credit rating. Such a person can also teach you new spending and saving patterns as a couple.

3. **Savings.** Let's face it, most Americans do not save much money—especially when they are just starting out. There is no doubt, however, that it is important to save money if one wants to own a home someday, send kids to college, or have a comfortable retirement. Even when you are just married, it is a good idea to get into the habit of trying to save some money. It may be especially advantageous, especially if you have two incomes, to save some money on a tax-deferred basis—either through a company pension plan or an individual retirement account. You should probably seek the advice of someone—parent, friend, accountant, banker—who can give you sound advice on these matters.

4. **Insurance.** Insurance is a protection against catastrophe. By pooling one's premiums with those of millions of others, you share the risk with them of something terrible happening. Thus you need health insurance. It is important that you have sufficient coverage without becoming "insurance poor" by trying to protect yourself against every eventuality, no matter how remote. Find a good insurance agent you can trust and listen to the advice he or she gives. Then make up your own minds together how much insurance you need and can afford.

5. Wills. Most newly married people do not want to face the possibility that one or both of them might die suddenly or tragically. They therefore put off making their will until "later." That later often turns into "never" and often leaves a grieving widow or widower to deal with a complex set of legal and financial problems. Get a lawyer, draw up your wills, and be done with it. Then put the wills in a safe place that a trusted family member knows. While you are doing your wills, also consider drawing up "living wills" or "durable power of attorney" for medical decisions. These allow your loved ones to know what your wishes are regarding medical treatment in case you are unable to decide for yourself.

6. Budgets. As a means of coordinating resources and expenditures, a budget is a financial plan that allows a couple to manage income sensibly and ensure their financial security. A well-planned and well-executed budget can help free both of you from worries over money and avoid many unhappy arguments. Adopt a first-year budget to suit your special circumstances as a couple (see pp. 56-57). Then see how it actually works out in practice and adapt it as you go along.

NUDEL

We invite you to play the **NUDEL** game, which should help you determine how closely you agree on the importance of the following items or services.

Consider each item, then check either: necessary, very useful, merely desirable, or extra luxury. In each column, check no more than nine items.

	Necessary	Useful	Desirable	Extra Luxury
VCR/Cable TV				
Microwave				
Health insurance				
A pet				
Savings account				
China; good dishes				
Personal computer				
Two-bedroom apartment				
Air conditioning				
Second car				
Stereo equipment				
Daily newspaper				
Dishwasher				
Two incomes				
Sewing machine				
Eating out once a week				
Health club membership				
A vacation each year				
Video games				
Credit cards				
Home ownership within ten years				
Continuing education courses				
Tickets to sports events and concerts				
Sports equipment such as skis				

KEEPING THINGS HUMMING

L ike money, how we spend our time at home is a measure of our commitments. There are many tasks that need to be done around the house in a marriage. Some of them are paid, most of them are not. Most of us have been raised to expect that certain jobs are done primarily by males and others done mostly by females. It might be good to be clear before you get married about who is going to do what.

Listed below are some common household chores. Working separately, mark under the correct column who you think should (S) and who you think will (W)—it's not always the same!—perform each task in your marriage. Then share the results with your partner. Discuss those areas where you have different ideas.

JOB	MALE	FEMALE	BOTH	EITHER	NEITHER	HIRE SOMEONE ELSE
Taking out the garbage						
Doing the dishes						
Making the bed						
Mowing the lawn						
Cooking dinner						
Vacuuming, dusting						
Scrubbing floors						
Washing windows						
Painting the house						
Making breakfast						
Grocery shopping						
Fixing the car						
Taking out the dog (cat)						
Ironing						
Preparing lunch						
Straightening the basement						
Keeping the checkbook						
Decorating the home						
Doing the laundry						
Cleaning the bathroom						
Gardening						
Shoveling snow						
Other: _____						
Other: _____						

NUDEL

We invite you to play the **NUDEL** game, which should help you determine how closely you agree on the importance of the following items or services.

Consider each item, then check either: necessary, very useful, merely desirable, or extra luxury. In each column, check no more than nine items.

	Necessary	Useful	Desirable	Extra Luxury
VCR/Cable TV				
Microwave				
Health insurance				
A pet				
Savings account				
China; good dishes				
Personal computer				
Two-bedroom apartment				
Air conditioning				
Second car				
Stereo equipment				
Daily newspaper				
Dishwasher				
Two incomes				
Sewing machine				
Eating out once a week				
Health club membership				
A vacation each year				
Video games				
Credit cards				
Home ownership within ten years				
Continuing education courses				
Tickets to sports events and concerts				
Sports equipment such as skis				

KEEPING THINGS HUMMING

Like money, how we spend our time at home is a measure of our commitments. There are many tasks that need to be done around the house in a marriage. Some of them are paid, most of them are not. Most of us have been raised to expect that certain jobs are done primarily by males and others done mostly by females. It might be good to be clear before you get married about who is going to do what.

Listed below are some common household chores. Working separately, mark under the correct column who you think should (S) and who you think will (W)—it's not always the same!—perform each task in your marriage. Then share the results with your partner. Discuss those areas where you have different ideas.

JOB	MALE	FEMALE	BOTH	EITHER	NEITHER	HIRE SOMEONE ELSE
Taking out the garbage	_____	_____	_____	_____	_____	_____
Doing the dishes	_____	_____	_____	_____	_____	_____
Making the bed	_____	_____	_____	_____	_____	_____
Mowing the lawn	_____	_____	_____	_____	_____	_____
Cooking dinner	_____	_____	_____	_____	_____	_____
Vacuuming, dusting	_____	_____	_____	_____	_____	_____
Scrubbing floors	_____	_____	_____	_____	_____	_____
Washing windows	_____	_____	_____	_____	_____	_____
Painting the house	_____	_____	_____	_____	_____	_____
Making breakfast	_____	_____	_____	_____	_____	_____
Grocery shopping	_____	_____	_____	_____	_____	_____
Fixing the car	_____	_____	_____	_____	_____	_____
Taking out the dog (cat)	_____	_____	_____	_____	_____	_____
Ironing	_____	_____	_____	_____	_____	_____
Preparing lunch	_____	_____	_____	_____	_____	_____
Straightening the basement	_____	_____	_____	_____	_____	_____
Keeping the checkbook	_____	_____	_____	_____	_____	_____
Decorating the home	_____	_____	_____	_____	_____	_____
Doing the laundry	_____	_____	_____	_____	_____	_____
Cleaning the bathroom	_____	_____	_____	_____	_____	_____
Gardening	_____	_____	_____	_____	_____	_____
Shoveling snow	_____	_____	_____	_____	_____	_____
Other: _____	_____	_____	_____	_____	_____	_____
Other: _____	_____	_____	_____	_____	_____	_____

OUR FAVORITE THINGS

Spouses in successful marriages learn to listen to each other with their ears, their eyes, their sense of touch. They are as aware of their partners' feelings as of what they say. They try to give all of their physical, psychological, and emotional attention to the other. Listening is critical to effective communication in marriage.

This exercise will help you understand how well you listen to and know your partner. If you have listened well over these months or years that you have known each other, you can probably guess what are your partner's ten favorite things to do.

Working alone, list the ten things you most enjoy doing. Then list the ten things you think your partner will put on his or her list. When you are finished, share your responses with each other. Where your lists do not agree, talk about the items. Maybe one of you has been too quiet about what you really enjoy, or maybe the other hasn't heard, or maybe you are still just getting to know each other. Have fun, and then plan some ways so that both of you can enjoy your favorite things.

MY FAVORITE THINGS

1. _____

2. _____

3. _____

4. _____

5. _____

6. _____

7. _____

8. _____

9. _____

10. _____

MY PARTNER'S FAVORITE THINGS

1. _____

2. _____

3. _____

4. _____

5. _____

6. _____

7. _____

8. _____

9. _____

10. _____

READ THE FUTURE

Although no one can accurately predict the future, couples who are able to look ahead, project their hopes and desires, and speculate on the possibilities that their life together holds are usually far more realistic. They are more flexible and better able to adapt to unusual events than those for whom every new experience is a shock or surprise.

Engage your imaginations—dream a little about the various stages of your marriage—and jot down short sentences or phrases that describe some of the features of your marriage as it might be in the second, seventh, fifteenth, and twenty-fifth years.

For each stage of married life indicated below, try to describe your life together as it might relate to children, career changes, family income, religious involvement, and changing goals. Compare your projections and discuss them.

SECOND YEAR

_____

_____

_____

_____

_____

_____

_____

SEVENTH YEAR

_____

_____

_____

_____

_____

_____

_____

FIFTEENTH YEAR

_____

_____

_____

_____

_____

_____

_____

TWENTY-FIFTH YEAR

_____

_____

_____

_____

_____

_____

_____

OUR FAVORITE THINGS

Spouses in successful marriages learn to listen to each other with their ears, their eyes, their sense of touch. They are as aware of their partners' feelings as of what they say. They try to give all of their physical, psychological, and emotional attention to the other. Listening is critical to effective communication in marriage.

This exercise will help you understand how well you listen to and know your partner. If you have listened well over these months or years that you have known each other, you can probably guess what are your partner's ten favorite things to do.

Working alone, list the ten things you most enjoy doing. Then list the ten things you think your partner will put on his or her list. When you are finished, share your responses with each other. Where your lists do not agree, talk about the items. Maybe one of you has been too quiet about what you really enjoy, or maybe the other hasn't heard, or maybe you are still just getting to know each other. Have fun, and then plan some ways so that both of you can enjoy your favorite things.

MY FAVORITE THINGS

1. _____

2. _____

3. _____

4. _____

5. _____

6. _____

7. _____

8. _____

9. _____

10. _____

MY PARTNER'S FAVORITE THINGS

1. _____

2. _____

3. _____

4. _____

5. _____

6. _____

7. _____

8. _____

9. _____

10. _____

READ THE FUTURE

Although no one can accurately predict the future, couples who are able to look ahead, project their hopes and desires, and speculate on the possibilities that their life together holds are usually far more realistic. They are more flexible and better able to adapt to unusual events than those for whom every new experience is a shock or surprise.

Engage your imaginations—dream a little about the various stages of your marriage—and jot down short sentences or phrases that describe some of the features of your marriage as it might be in the second, seventh, fifteenth, and twenty-fifth years.

For each stage of married life indicated below, try to describe your life together as it might relate to children, career changes, family income, religious involvement, and changing goals. Compare your projections and discuss them.

SECOND YEAR

_____

_____

_____

_____

_____

_____

_____

_____

SEVENTH YEAR

_____

_____

_____

_____

_____

_____

_____

_____

FIFTEENTH YEAR

_____

_____

_____

_____

_____

_____

_____

_____

TWENTY-FIFTH YEAR

_____

_____

_____

_____

_____

_____

_____

_____